FAITH

LIKE A

CHILD

**The Lessons Children
Teach Us About Trusting God**

Eunike Smith

FAITH LIKE A CHILD
Published by Pure Wish Publishing

Copyright © 2025 by Eunike Smith
ISBN-13: 979-8-9993313-1-1

Printed in the United States of America

Dedication

For everyone learning to believe again.

Acknowledgments

This book was written with many sleepless nights, much prayer, and countless moments of quiet wonder and it wouldn't exist without the people who reflect Jesus to me every day.

To my husband, Jonathan, thank you for showing me what the love of Christ looks like in everyday life. Your quiet strength, servant heart, and steadfast faith are a living example of what it means to walk like Jesus. I am endlessly grateful to share this life's journey with you.

To my precious children, Chessy and Leon, you are the heartbeat of these pages. Your faith, your laughter, your pure and open hearts have taught me more about God than any sermon ever could. Thank you for reminding me, daily, what it looks like to trust fully and love freely.

To the readers, thank you for opening your heart to these simple stories. My prayer is that through them, you are drawn closer to the Father's arms, and that you remember: you are still His child, and He delights in you.

Above all, to Jesus, this book is Yours. Every word, every lesson, every whisper of grace, may it point back to You, the One who holds me when I fall, lifts me when I'm weary, and calls me Your own.

Contents

Introduction

"Truly I tell you, unless you change and become like little
children, you will never enter the kingdom of heaven."
—Matthew 18:3

There is something profoundly beautiful in the way a child
believes. A child doesn't demand to see the blueprint before
trusting the builder. They don't analyze the science behind
rainbows before being delighted by them. A child believes even
if they don't understand everything, because they trust in a
greater design and purpose.

Jesus, in all His wisdom, pointed to children—not
scholars, not kings, not even seasoned disciples—as the
example of the kind of faith that opens the door to His
Kingdom. This wasn't a call to ignorance, but to innocence.
Not to immaturity, but to wonder. Not to blind belief, but to
wholehearted trust.

This book is an invitation to rediscover that kind of faith.
The kind that jumps into the arms of the Father without
hesitation. The kind that believes He is good, even when the
path is unclear. The kind that listens for His voice in the quiet
and expects Him to speak.

Whether your faith feels tired and tangled, or strong and
steady, may these pages help you return—not to where you

once were, but to who you were always meant to be: a beloved child of God, resting in His love, trusting in His promises, and walking with Him in simple, courageous faith.

Let's journey back together. Back to wonder. Back to trust. Back to childlike faith.

CHAPTER 1

When Trust Took Flight

I still remember the way my daughter Chessy used to leap into my arms without warning. No countdown. No hesitation. Just a full-body launch into the unknown with complete confidence that I'd catch her.

Once, she jumped before I was even looking. I had turned to grab something, and in that split second, she took off. I caught her midair, just in time, my heart pounding in my chest. I held her tightly, still catching my breath, while she laughed in delight, utterly calm, completely unafraid.

She didn't question. She didn't doubt. She didn't calculate. In her eyes, I was strong enough, fast enough, trustworthy enough. Always.

That moment never left me. It became more than a memory. It became a mirror, reflecting the kind of faith I once had... and the kind I long to have again.

When Faith Starts to Hesitate

I didn't always hesitate. There was a time in my life when I prayed with boldness, stepped out freely, and believed God would show up simply because He said He would. I didn't overthink, overanalyze, or let fear stop me.

But somewhere along the way, life chipped away at that confidence. Disappointments lingered longer than expected. Prayers went unanswered—or so I thought. Doors closed. People walked away. Dreams slipped through my hands. And without realizing it, I started playing it safe. I began asking, "What if?"

What if it doesn't work? What if I heard Him wrong? What if I fall, and no one catches me this time?

My faith shifted from daring to calculating. From surrendered to skeptical. I stopped leaping.

Hesitating faith doesn't always look like rebellion. Sometimes, it looks like silence where there once was song. Like double-checking instead of declaring. Like praying safe prayers instead of bold ones. Like building backup plans "just in case" God doesn't come through. And often, it comes quietly. It disguises itself as maturity. But it's not maturity—it's fear, dressed up as wisdom.

The truth is, some of us are walking around with tired faith. Worn down not because we stopped believing in God, but because we quietly started wondering if He's still listening. If He'll still show up.

Peter looked down, too. He stepped out of the boat with the wildness of childlike faith, eyes on Jesus. For a moment, he walked on water. Until he didn't.

> "But when he saw the wind, he was afraid and, beginning to sink, cried out, 'Lord, save me!'"
> —Matthew 14:30

He looked down. He noticed the waves. He panicked. He sank. He let fear outweigh trust. And yet, Jesus didn't let him drown. That's what I love most about that story. Yes, Peter hesitated. Yes, he started to sink. But Jesus still reached out and caught him. That moment tells the truth about Jesus: His rescue isn't delayed by our doubt.

Jesus knows we hesitate. Jesus isn't surprised by our hesitation. He is not surprised by our shaky steps. He doesn't flinch at our fear. He meets us right there. Like the desperate father who brought his demon-possessed son to Jesus:

> "I believe; help my unbelief!"
> —Mark 9:24

It wasn't polished. It wasn't perfect. But it was honest. Sometimes the most powerful prayer we can pray is,
> "I believe, but I'm scared."
> "I want to trust, but I'm struggling."

"I want to jump again, Jesus. Help me."

And He does. Not with scolding, but with mercy. Not with demands, but with open arms.

Faith isn't always walking perfectly. Sometimes, faith is sinking and still crying out.

How Children Teach Us to Trust

Jesus once said,

> "Truly I tell you, unless you change and become like little children, you will never enter the kingdom of heaven."
> —Matthew 18:3

At first, that sounds like a strange requirement. Children can be loud, messy, impulsive, but that's not what Jesus was praising. He was pointing to their purity of trust, their quick forgiveness, their hunger to learn, and their absolute confidence in the one who cares for them. They believe—not because they have all the answers, but because they know who they belong to.

That's how Chessy lived. She didn't leap into my arms because she had tested my reflexes or done a risk assessment. She jumped because she knew me. Her confidence wasn't in her landing—it was in my love. And that's what God is calling us back to. Not blind naivety, but bold familiarity. Not recklessness, but reliance. He's not asking us to be foolish—just faithful.

Relearning the Leap

These days, I find myself standing at the edge more often than I'd like to admit. I see the gap between what I know and what I hope for... and I freeze.

I wonder if I'll fall.

I wonder if God will really show up.

I wonder if I'm foolish to even try.

But then, I remember Chessy's face—carefree, secure, joyful. Not because she knew the outcome, but because she knew the one who waited for her. And I whisper, "God, help me leap like that again. Help me trust You without the need for a five-step plan. Help me run to You without waiting for a sign. Help me jump—not because I'm sure of the landing, but because I'm sure of You."

The truth is, God has never missed a single catch. Not once. Even in seasons where I thought I was falling, I landed in His grace. Sometimes it didn't look the way I expected. Sometimes it took longer than I wanted. But He was there. Every time. And I want to live like I believe that again.

Because when we leap with childlike faith—without a backup plan, without looking down—we don't just fall. We fall into grace. A grace that holds. A grace that steadies. A grace that always catches.

Maybe you've stopped leaping, too. Maybe life has made you cautious. Maybe your heart still bears the bruises of hopes deferred. Maybe you're holding yourself back because you're tired of being let down.

But Jesus is calling you back to the edge. Back to trust. Back to joy. Back to the leap. He's standing below, arms wide open. Not demanding perfection. Just inviting surrender. He's not asking you to jump without fear. He's asking you to jump anyway—because you trust Him.

So here's to leaping again. Here's to the kind of trust that doesn't wait for the perfect moment. The kind of faith that jumps, midair, smiling, because it knows it will be caught.

This journey of faith is not about having all the answers. It's about remembering who waits for you at the bottom. And saying yes, not because you know the landing, but because you know the One who will catch you. All it takes... is one brave leap.

A Prayer for the Leap of Faith

Father,
Thank You for being the One who never misses a catch.
When fear holds me back, remind me of the trust I once had—
the kind that jumps without hesitation, simply because I know
You're there.

Help me leap again.
Not because I'm certain of the outcome,
but because I'm sure of You.
Teach me to trust like a child,
to rest in Your arms and to walk in simple, surrendered
faith.

I know You'll catch me.
Every time.

Amen.

CHAPTER 2

The Cry in the Midnight Hour

It was just after midnight when I heard him. That unmistakable sound—a sharp, sudden wail that pierced the silence of the house. My three-month-old son was awake and wailing. My eyes opened instantly. My body moved before my mind could fully catch up.

Leon was crying. He was hungry, tired, or maybe just in need of comfort. At three months old, he had no other way of expressing what he felt. He didn't know the words for hunger or fear. He didn't know how to explain his needs or articulate his pain. All he knew was to cry—to call out.

And as soon as I heard him, I went. I scooped him up from his crib, pressed his little body to my chest, and whispered softly, "I'm here. I've got you." His cries quieted almost immediately. Not because the need was gone, but because I was there.

He didn't need the problem fixed right away. He just needed presence. He didn't know what would happen next. He just knew he wasn't alone. And as I rocked him in the dark, I heard the whisper of the Spirit: "This is what I want your faith to look like." Not put together. Not wordy or wise. Just honest. Dependent. Real.

Faith Doesn't Always Have the Words

Leon didn't have language, but he had trust. He cried, not because he understood everything, but because he knew I would come.

There was something so pure in that moment. So vulnerable and unfiltered. It struck me deeply: this is the faith Jesus calls us to. Not eloquent. Not rehearsed. Just the kind that cries out and trusts someone will answer.

So often I've tried to come to God with the "right" words. The steady tone. The strong prayer. But God isn't moved by my performance. He's moved by my heart.

In Scripture, faith is rarely tidy. It's raw. Unfiltered. Like a child crying in the night. Time and time again, God responds.

Psalm 34:17 says,

"The righteous cry out, and the Lord hears them;
He delivers them from all their troubles."

It doesn't say the righteous pray perfectly. It says they cry. Sometimes faith isn't a shout. It's a sigh. A whisper. A breath that barely makes it out. It's the soul saying, "Father, I need You."

Leon couldn't solve his need. And the truth is neither can I. But I don't have to. God never asked me to. Instead, He invites me to call out. To cry, not as a failure of faith—but as an act of it.

As a mother, I don't rush to my son's side because he uses the right words. I come because I love him. His cry moves me. His need draws me near. It doesn't matter if he's able to explain what's wrong or articulate what he needs. The moment I hear his voice tremble, I'm on my way. Not because he earned it. Not because he asked perfectly. But simply because I love him and he's mine.

And the breathtaking truth of the Gospel is this: God feels the same about us. He doesn't wait for us to tidy up our prayers or wrap our requests in eloquence. He responds to our groans. He draws near to our weakness. When all we can offer is just tears—He listens. He moves.

In Exodus 2:23–25, we read that the Israelites groaned under slavery in Egypt. They didn't offer grand prayers. They simply cried out. And the Scripture says, "God heard their groaning..."

God didn't wait for perfect words. He moved because He loved them and they were His.

15

When Faith Sounds Like Tears

That night, Leon reminded me: faith doesn't always sound peaceful. Sometimes, it sounds like a cry in the dark.

We don't often think of crying as faith. We think of it as weakness, as breaking, as not having enough. But what if crying is the bravest thing we can offer? To cry is to reach. To cry is to admit our need. It's the heart's way of saying, "I can't do this alone." And in God's eyes, that is faith.

The Israelites groaned in Egypt, and God heard them. Hannah wept in the temple, and God answered her. David cried out from the caves, and God drew near. Even Jesus, in Gethsemane, wept and was heard. Crying is not the absence of faith. It is a form of it. A fragile, trembling faith that still believes someone is listening. Still hopes someone will come.

When all you have left is your tears, and you lift them to heaven, that is worship. That is trust. That is faith, raw and real. And the beautiful truth? God never ignores a single tear. Not one.

I don't know when I stopped crying out like that. When I started thinking I needed to clean up my heart before coming to Him. That my weakness made me unworthy of His presence. But God doesn't come because we impress Him. He comes because we're His. He comes because He hears. Because He's moved. Because He's near.

There are moments when theology won't fix the ache. Moments when all we can do is whisper, groan, or cry in the

16

dark. But that's enough. Because childlike faith doesn't try to carry the weight. It simply reaches out to the One who can.

If you've been holding it in, trying to be strong, trying to be spiritual, or trying to hold your breath and your world together, this is your invitation. Let go. Cry out. You don't need to explain the pain or have the plan. You just need to cry and trust that He is coming. Not always with quick fixes, but always with Himself. Because God doesn't just want to answer your prayer. He wants to hold you through it. And like Leon resting safely in my arms that night, you can breathe again. Not because everything's okay, but because you're not alone. You're held. You're heard. You're loved.

So let the tears fall. Let your voice tremble. Let your faith sound like a midnight cry. He hears you. And He's already on His way.

A Prayer from the Crib

Father,
I don't have the words tonight.
My heart is tired, my faith feels small.
But I know You are near.

I cry out to You—not in fear,
but in faith that You are the God who hears.
The God who runs to me.
The God who picks me up and holds me close.

Let my tears speak what I cannot.
Let my breath be enough.
Let Your arms be the place I rest.
I trust You.

Amen.

Even when you can't explain the pain, God understands the cry—and He comes, simply because you're His.

CHAPTER 3

The Children Who Came to Jesus

Not long after that night with Leon, I found myself lingering over a familiar passage in Mark:

> "People were bringing little children to Jesus for Him to place His hands on them, but the disciples rebuked them."
> —Mark 10:13

I paused right there. I tried to imagine the scene. The sound of little sandals slapping dusty paths. The shuffle of parents moving forward, some hesitant, others hopeful. The nervous smiles of mothers wondering, Will He bless my child too? Some of them may have carried infants in their arms, while others knelt beside wide-eyed toddlers clinging to their legs.

And then—rebuke. The disciples stepped in. Maybe they crossed their arms, shook their heads, gently waved the parents away. Maybe it started with polite discouragement, then firmer tones.

"He's too busy."

"This isn't the time."

"This is serious business. He's teaching important things."

Their intentions may have been protective. But in trying to shield Jesus from the "interruption," they silenced something sacred.

"When Jesus saw this, He was indignant."
—Mark 10:14a

That word grabbed me. Indignant. Not annoyed. Not disappointed. Not mildly disapproving. Indignant. The kind of anger that rises when something beautiful is being threatened. The kind of fire that burns in the heart of someone fiercely protective of what truly matters.

Jesus wasn't upset because His schedule was disrupted. He was grieved because the children were being kept from His presence. The ones with the most uncluttered faith—the purest desire to draw near—were being told they didn't belong. And so He spoke—not gently, but with fire in His voice:

"'Let the little children come to Me, and do not hinder them, for the kingdom of God belongs to such as these.'"
—Mark 10:14b

Let them come. Don't hinder them. Don't overcomplicate what was always meant to be simple. Don't build fences around the open arms of God. Don't tell the tired, the small, the messy, the dependent that they need to "wait their turn." Jesus didn't just allow the children. He defended them. He honored them. He lifted them up as the very model of what it means to belong in His kingdom.

He Made Room

The disciples thought they were doing the right thing. Maybe they were trying to preserve order. Protect Jesus' time. Shield Him from what looked like chaos—sticky hands, loud giggles, little feet that didn't understand reverence. In their minds, they were guarding authority. But they misunderstood His heart. They thought authority meant distance. That to be sacred was to be separate. That Jesus belonged to the clean, the quiet, the qualified. But Jesus showed them something truer and deeper: Love doesn't push away. Love makes room.

He wasn't bothered by the interruption. He was brokenhearted by the barrier. Because what they saw as distraction, He saw as excitement. What they dismissed as

23

childish, He received as worship. To Jesus, the children weren't getting in the way of ministry. They were the ministry. They didn't need to earn His time. They didn't need to meet a standard. They just needed to come. And He made space—right in the middle of everything—to welcome them. No appointment. No qualifications. Just open arms.

The Simplicity of Trust

Why was Jesus so passionate about letting the children come? Because they knew something we forget. They didn't come to earn anything. They came because they were drawn. Drawn to something safe. Drawn to Someone good. They didn't analyze the theology. Didn't worry about appearances. Didn't stop to ask if they were worthy. They just came—without hesitation. Without needing a reason or rehearsing their request or wondering if they were too much. They came not with arguments, but with arms outstretched. Because that's what trust does. It doesn't need all the answers. It doesn't wait until the fear is gone. It just moves toward the One who feels like home.

That's why Jesus said, "The kingdom of God belongs to such as these." Not because they had it all figured out. But because they were willing to come empty. Because they trusted He would fill.

The kingdom is not inherited by the impressive. It is received by the dependent. By the ones who don't just believe with their minds, but lean in with their hearts. The ones who don't perform to be noticed, they simply want to be near. That's the kind of trust Jesus holds up and says, This—this is what I'm looking for.

When We "Grow Up" Too Much

Somewhere along the way, we forget how to be small. We trade simplicity for strategy. We learn how to impress, how to perform, how to hide what hurts. We tuck away our questions. We manage our expectations. We polish ourselves before we pray. And we call it maturity. But underneath all that spiritual adulthood... is a quiet ache for something we've lost.

We replace dependence with self-sufficiency. Vulnerability with filtered, curated strength. We start to believe the lie that God loves us more when we're composed. That He listens better when we're tidy. That faith is proved by how little we need, not how freely we come needing everything.

But Jesus never asked us to outgrow childlike faith. He never looked at the children in Mark 10 and said,

"Come back when you understand more."

"Come back when you're quieter, cleaner, better behaved."

He received them just as they were. No pretense, no performance, no perfection required. And then He turned to the adults and said: "You want to belong in the kingdom? Become like them." Not because children are innocent, but because they are honest. They cry when they're sad. They reach when they're afraid. They ask bold questions and expect to be answered. They don't second-guess their welcome.

And maybe that's the truest kind of faith: Not the kind that never doubts, but the kind that dares to come anyway.

The Kingdom Belongs to the Dependent

Jesus didn't say the kingdom includes children. He said it belongs to them. That's a bold claim. It means childlike faith isn't a cute metaphor—it's a requirement. A doorway. A map. In His upside-down kingdom, it's not the powerful who inherit the promise. It's the dependent. The small. The ones who know they need Him. And that turns everything on its head. Because we've been taught to hide our weakness. To lead with our strengths. To keep the trembling parts tucked away where no one can see.

But in the kingdom of God? Weakness isn't something to hide. It's the very door we walk through. Need isn't something to be ashamed of. It's something to bring. Tears aren't a sign of failure. They're a language He understands. We don't come because we've earned access. We come because He's made a way. We don't come because we've achieved something. We come because He has. We don't come because we've figured it all out. We come because He is the answer.

And when we do, when we drop the act, when we stop striving and simply run to Him as we are—we find arms already open. We find the same welcome those children found on the dusty road that day. Not just permission to draw near, but delight at our arrival.

So let the children lead us. Let their trust soften our grown-up defenses. Let their simplicity silence our spiritual striving. Let their wide-eyed wonder call us back to a faith that runs free. Because Jesus isn't waiting for you to prove yourself. He's waiting for you to come. Not cleaned up. Not ready. Just real. Just His.

A Prayer to Come Freely

Jesus,
Help me come to You with nothing to prove.
No masks, no polished prayers—just me.
Messy. Honest. Bare.

Like a child runs to a loving parent,
let me run to You without hesitation,
believing You welcome me just as I am.
Not cleaned up. Not put together. Just loved.

Draw me into Your presence,
where fear fades and love remains.
Speak peace over the chaos inside me.
And gently remind me—You're not waiting for perfection,
You're just waiting for me.

Amen

Childlike faith doesn't wait to be worthy—
it simply runs to the One who welcomes.

CHAPTER 4

The Reach That Brought Me Near

It happened on an ordinary afternoon. There were no halos of light streaming through the windows. No music playing in the background. Just the soft rhythm of domestic life—the hum of the dryer, the faint tick of the clock, the comforting rustle of laundry being folded.

Leon had just woken from his nap, cheeks warm with sleep and the faint imprint of the blanket still pressed against his skin. He blinked in that slow, dazed way babies do, as though adjusting to the light of a world they'd momentarily forgotten.

I was only a few steps away, folding a pile of warm clothes, when I felt the stillness between us shift. I looked up to see his gaze—locked on me, full of wonder, recognition, and longing. His hands twitched, legs kicked, and then he smiled... that gummy, irresistible smile only babies can give.

And then, without hesitation, he reached. Tiny arms stretched outward, body tipping slightly forward with the effort. It was not graceful. It was not sure. But it was full of something pure and powerful. He reached for me. He didn't know how to get there. His muscles hadn't yet mastered crawling or walking. He didn't calculate distance or effort. He simply knew I was close. And that was enough. He trusted I would come. So I did.

I dropped the laundry mid-fold, closing the gap with a few quick steps, and scooped him into my arms. He giggled, burying his face in my shoulder like he had found what he'd been looking for. And I whispered into his ear, "You knew I'd come, didn't you?" Because he did. He never doubted his worth. He never paused to question if I was too busy. He didn't analyze the space between us or try to earn the embrace. He simply reached, and believed love would meet him.

Leon's reach was small. But it changed everything in that moment. There were no words. No striving. Just the honest movement of a heart that trusted love would draw near. And in that still, sacred moment, I sensed the Spirit whisper: That—right there—is faith. Not the kind that makes grand declarations. Not the kind that walks tall with confidence. But the kind that leans, stretches, hopes. The kind that dares to lift trembling hands even when unsure. The kind that trusts someone stronger is within reach. The kind that doesn't know how, but believes He will come.

God doesn't respond to polish. He responds to presence. To the raw reach of a childlike heart. To the sigh too deep for words. To the silent prayer on tear-stained pillows. To the glance heavenward that says, "Are You still there?" And every time, He comes close.

The Woman Who Reached

Leon's reach stirred the memory of another, a woman from the Gospels whose story still echoes. She had been bleeding for twelve long years. Twelve years of isolation. Of being called unclean. Twelve years of doctors and disappointments. Of waiting rooms and whispered prayers. Of being overlooked, forgotten, dismissed. Her body had grown weary. Her soul, threadbare. But when she heard that Jesus was passing by, something within her stirred.

She didn't make a scene. She didn't call out. She didn't even ask. She simply reached.

> "She came up behind Him and touched the edge of His cloak, and immediately her bleeding stopped. 'Who touched Me?' Jesus asked... Then He said to her, 'Daughter, your faith has healed you. Go in peace.'"
> —Luke 8:44—48

She reached not because she felt strong, but because she was desperate. She didn't step boldly; she crawled quietly through the crowd. But Jesus noticed. In a sea of people, He saw her. Her fingers brushed the hem of heaven. And that was enough.

Her faith didn't shout. It didn't wave flags or make demands. It whispered,

"If I could just touch Him..."

And Heaven responded.

Faith Isn't Always Loud

We often think faith is supposed to look bold. A steady voice. A firm stance. A confident prayer. But sometimes, faith is quiet. Sometimes, faith is whispering His name in the dark. Sometimes, it's dragging yourself to church with nothing left to give. Sometimes, it's opening your Bible and saying, "Please... say something." Sometimes, it's simply staying when everything in you wants to run.

Faith can be messy. Faith can tremble. Faith can look like reaching with hands that don't feel holy. And yet, God sees it all. He's not waiting for the moment we feel unshakable. He moves toward us the moment we stretch.

Maybe today your reach feels weak. Maybe your prayers are softer than you'd like. Maybe you're wondering if God even notices. But here's the truth: He does. He is not measuring your effort. He is not waiting for eloquence. He is not comparing you to anyone else. He is simply waiting for you to reach. You don't need to have the strength to stand. You don't have to cross the whole room. You don't even have to speak. You just have to lift your heart. Like a baby reaching through the quiet. Like a woman brushing against His robe. Like a child stretching toward her Father.

And when you do, He comes. He closes the distance. He scoops you up. He holds you close. And He whispers, "You knew I'd come, didn't you?"

A Prayer to Be Met

Father,
Sometimes I feel like I don't know how to move forward.
But You're not asking me to take every step alone—
You're just asking me to reach.

So here I am.
Arms stretched, heart open.
Come meet me here, like You always do.

Amen.

Faith isn't about how strong your reach is—
it's about knowing Who to reach for.

CHAPTER 5

The Boy Who Gave His Lunch

The hillside was alive with sound. Children's laughter echoed between rocks and tree branches, mingling with the murmurs of families gathering. There was the shuffle of tired feet, the creak of woven baskets on backs, the occasional bray of a donkey, and underneath it all—a low hum of expectation.

They had come from everywhere. Dusty roads told of long walks under the sun. Worn sandals padded across the dry earth. Parents carried little ones on their hips or shoulders. Grandparents leaned on walking sticks. Neighbors came together, huddled in small groups, whispering about what they had heard. Because He was there. Jesus. The man who had healed the sick, spoken with authority, and touched lepers with compassion. The man who didn't just teach about God but revealed Him—with every word, every look, every touch. And now they followed Him—not just out of curiosity, but out of something deeper. Hunger. Not just the kind that rumbles in the stomach, but the kind that aches in the soul. They had tasted a glimpse of something eternal, and they wanted more. He had healed them. He had taught them. He had seen them.

But as the sun climbed higher in the sky and shadows began to shorten, the hunger in their spirits was joined by a hunger in their bellies. Children began to tug at their mothers' sleeves. Fathers glanced around, eyes scanning for food vendors that didn't exist. The crowd grew restless. The air shifted. And quietly, anxiety crept in.

The disciples noticed it first. They looked out over the endless sea of faces—thousands of them—and felt the pressure mount. No towns nearby. No shops. No supplies. And not nearly enough money to buy food even if there had been. So they brought their practical suggestion to Jesus. "Send them away," they said. "Let them go find food before it's too late." It wasn't cruel. It made sense. They were thinking logically, even compassionately. Trying to solve the problem the best way they knew how. But Jesus wasn't anxious. He wasn't overwhelmed by the crowd or caught off guard by the need. He looked at them with calm, confident eyes and said something unexpected:

"You give them something to eat."
—Matthew 14:16

I can almost picture the disciples' confusion. The shared glances, the raised eyebrows. Feed them? With what? They

40

began to search, peering through the crowd, asking questions, scanning for anything or anyone with food to spare.

And then, a boy. He wasn't loud. He wasn't pushy. He didn't stand on tiptoe or wave his hands to get attention. He was simply there—a quiet figure holding something small. Five barley loaves. Two little fish. Probably packed by a mother who loved him. Maybe she reminded him not to forget to eat. Maybe she kissed his forehead that morning, never imagining that her simple act of care would become part of a miracle.

He stepped forward. Not because he had plenty. Not because he had answers. Not because he was told to. But because he had something, and he was willing to give it. And that—that was enough.

He Gave What He Had

This moment humbles me every time I read it. The boy didn't wait to be noticed. He didn't need a guarantee that it would work. He didn't think, "This isn't much... it probably won't help." He just gave. Freely. Quietly. Completely. Five barley loaves—coarse bread made for the poor, not the elite. Two small fish—likely dried, more of a snack than a meal.

It wasn't impressive. It wasn't abundant. But it was real. It was what he had, and he offered it with open hands. And Jesus didn't critique it. He didn't ask for more. He didn't turn it away. He took it.

That's the kind of faith that touches heaven. The kind that doesn't wait for significance to step in. The kind that doesn't wait for abundance to begin. The kind that offers the small and ordinary, trusting it will be enough in the hands of God.

Jesus didn't need a banquet. He needed a yes. He lifted the offering toward heaven. Gave thanks. And then He broke it.

Then He broke it again.

And again.

And again.

Each breaking became a beginning. Each piece became provision. Each moment in His hands became more than it was before. Baskets began to fill. Hands began to pass. The crowd that once murmured with hunger now sat in growing wonder. And everyone ate. Not just a bite. Not just a taste. They were satisfied. Every man. Every woman. Every child. And twelve baskets of leftovers remained, more than they began with. Abundance poured from surrender. Overflow poured from trust.

Can you imagine the boy's eyes? Watching his little lunch move from hand to hand... Watching what once belonged to him become nourishment for strangers... Watching Jesus multiply the very thing he was willing to release...

He didn't preach. He didn't lead. He didn't plan a revival. He gave his lunch. And heaven met his offering with miracle. No spotlight. No applause. No name mentioned in Scripture. Just quiet obedience and eternal impact. Because when we say yes to Jesus, our little becomes legacy. Our simple becomes sacred. And our willingness becomes a window for God's glory.

This story isn't really about food. It's about faith. It's about how God moves when we offer what we have, even when it feels too small. It's about how He doesn't need us to be perfect—He just needs us to be present. It's about how childlike faith doesn't hold back, waiting until it feels "important enough" to matter. It simply trusts.

God doesn't wait for grand gestures. He responds to surrendered ones. Your weary prayer. Your tired service. Your quiet faithfulness. He sees it all. And He multiplies what's placed in His hands.

The disciples saw a crowd, and panicked. The boy saw Jesus, and believed. The disciples calculated what was missing. The boy trusted Jesus. That's the gift of childlike faith: It doesn't obsess over limitations. It recognizes presence. It doesn't say, "We don't have enough." It says, "Here's what I have. Use it."

When One Yes Feeds a Thousand

This is the part that lingers: The boy didn't just feed himself. He fed a multitude. His yes became nourishment. His surrender became a miracle with ripple effects. Because faith is never just for us. Your trust may be the reason someone else finds hope. Your yes may be the breakthrough someone else has been praying for.

Jesus could have called down manna from heaven. He could have created a feast from nothing. But instead, He used a child. He used someone small, someone quiet, someone with very little to give, and showed us what He can do with a heart that says, "It's Yours."

So what's in your hands today? It might feel like barley loaves and dried fish. Ordinary. Inadequate. Forgettable. But in the hands of Jesus? It's more than enough.

A Prayer to Offer What's in My Hands

Jesus,
So often I hold back because I think what I have isn't enough.
But You never asked me to be enough
You only asked me to give.

Teach me to trust You like that little boy did.
Help me bring what I have,
no matter how small,
and place it in Your hands.

Amen.

CHAPTER 6

Wonder in His Eyes

It was one of those slow mornings—calm, quiet, and kind. The kind that feels like a deep breath you didn't know you needed. Like grace showing up before you even asked. Golden light threaded its way through the windows, warming the floorboards and whispering the day awake. The hum of stillness lingered in the air, untouched by to-do lists or headlines. The world, in that moment, was gentle.

Leon had just risen from sleep. His hair was tousled and sticking up in places, cheeks still carrying the pink blush of dreams. His breath, slow and steady against my shoulder. His little body melted into mine like only a child's can—completely unguarded, fully trusting, wholly content.

I carried him through the hallway, arms wrapped around him like a prayer. It was nothing special, just a slow morning, a familiar rhythm, a mother with her son.

But then, he saw it. We passed the front window, and something caught his eye. Sunlight. Not just light, but alive light—flickering through the trees like heaven breathing through the branches. The wind carried the leaves in a slow, swaying dance. Shadows played on the glass, rising and falling like a lullaby for the eyes. And in an instant, he stopped. His small body stilled. His breath caught. And those sleepy eyes grew wide with awe.

He didn't point. He didn't speak. He didn't explain. He simply watched. Like the world had cracked open and glory was spilling through the branches. It was nothing spectacular by grown-up standards. No fireworks. No grand display. No thunderous voice from heaven. Just light and leaves and a breeze. But to him, it was wonder. And to me, it was precious.

The Quiet Language of Wonder

Before a child learns to talk, they learn to see. Before they speak in questions, they live in response. Before they pray with words, they praise with wonder.

Leon didn't analyze the moment. He didn't ask, "Why do the leaves move?" or "What makes the light dance?" He didn't dissect the science behind beauty. He didn't try to understand it—he received it. Like a gift. Like it was enough. Because it was.

Children are fluent in the first language of heaven. They don't need a worship leader to cue their hearts. They don't need reasons to rejoice. They just haven't forgotten how. They notice. They linger. They wonder. And in doing so, they draw near to the God who laced wonder into every corner of the world.

Matthew 5:8 says,

"Blessed are the pure in heart, for they shall see God."

Not the clever, Not the strong, Not the highly educated or deeply religious, but the pure in heart. The unjaded. The unhurried. The ones with eyes still soft enough to see the sacred in the ordinary.

God hides Himself in plain sight, you know. He whispers through leaves. He sings in birdsong. He paints with light. And He waits—in the quiet corners, in the overlooked details, in the moments we too often race past.

Wonder doesn't require a spotlight. It doesn't shout for attention. It waits—gently, patiently—asking only, "Will you stop long enough to see Me?"

But somewhere along the way, we forget. We grow up. Grow busy. Grow blind. We trade curiosity for cynicism. Trade pauses for plans. Trade "Wow!" for "What's next?" We don't mean to, but we lose the eyes to see. We scroll past beauty. We silence mystery with logic. We forget that stillness is sacred. That quiet is not empty, it's full. That God still walks in gardens and whispers through trees. We stop looking. But He hasn't stopped showing up.

The Stillness That Holds Glory

That morning, I didn't rush Leon. Didn't tug him along or break the silence. I watched him watch. And in the stillness, I felt the hush of heaven lean in. "This is worship, too," the Spirit whispered. Not loud. Not scripted. Not tied to music or words. Just a gaze that lingers. A breath that slows. A heart that whispers, "You're here."

Sometimes, faith looks like movement. Sometimes, it looks like prayer. But sometimes—it just looks like wonder. The kind that sees the world bathed in God-light.

What if wonder is how we find our way home again? What if childlike faith isn't just about believing harder, but noticing deeper? Noticing the beauty. The nearness. The unexpected holiness hiding in plain sight. Noticing Him.

Because the light still dances. The leaves still praise. Creation still sings. And God, He still walks among us. We just need to slow down. Open our eyes. Lift our gaze. Pause long enough to wonder. And maybe, just maybe, you'll see Him standing right there, in the shimmer of morning light, waiting for your eyes to open. And like my son that morning—stand still in the arms of a Father, and see.

Leon didn't need a sermon that day. The sunlight preached just fine.

A Prayer to See Again

Father,
My eyes are tired.
My heart too hurried.

But I want to see again,
to slow down,
to look up,
to let wonder in.

Teach me to see like a child,
to let Your light move me,
even in quiet places.

Wake my soul with beauty.
And let wonder lead me to You.

Amen.

CHAPTER 7

Because She Knows She's Loved

"Mom, can I have a fairy bedroom?"

I looked up from the laundry basket, sock in one hand, the smell of fresh cotton still in the air. And there she was, Chessy, bright-eyed and barefoot, standing beside me with her phone in hand and excitement in her voice. She had already curated a dream. A collection of images—soft lights, floral wallpaper, a canopy bed that looked like it belonged in an enchanted forest. There were vines strung with twinkle lights, cloud-shaped pillows, and pastel tones that shimmered like a sunset dipped in magic.

There was no hesitation in her question. No trembling. No shame in her asking. Just pure, unfiltered hope, because she already knew the answer to the deeper question:

Am I loved enough to be heard?

She didn't ask from fear. She asked from love. She asked because she believes that love leans in. And it wasn't just that one question. Chessy's heart is a wellspring of dreams, ideas, and desires, and she holds nothing back:

"Mom, can I have a roller blade?"
"Mom, can I have a sticker?"
"Mom, can I have pimple patches?"
"Mom, can I have a dog?"

Each request, no matter how whimsical or wild, comes with the same tone: Hopeful. Confident. Unfiltered. She knows that love isn't measured by how many wishes are granted, but by the safety of being allowed to ask. And that's exactly the kind of faith Jesus calls us to.

Always Welcome

Children don't edit their prayers. They don't try to sound spiritual. They just ask.

When Jesus said, "Let the little children come to me and do not hinder them, for the kingdom of heaven belongs to such as these" (Matthew 19:14). He wasn't just making space for toddlers on His lap—He was inviting all of us back to that fearless posture of trust.

Children ask because they believe someone cares. They believe love listens. They believe in welcome before answers.

And Jesus does welcome. He doesn't roll His eyes at your requests. He doesn't sigh in disappointment when you show up again with the same prayer. He welcomes you.

In Luke 11:9-10, Jesus says:
"Ask and it will be given to you;
seek and you will find;
knock and the door will be opened to you.
For everyone who asks receives;
the one who seeks finds;
and to the one who knocks, the door will be opened."

Do you notice the tone in His words? There's no hesitation. No irritation. Only invitation. Jesus doesn't just tolerate your asking—He encourages it. He expects it. Because prayer isn't just about receiving something from God; it's about drawing near to Him.

And yes, sometimes the answer is "Yes". Sometimes it's "No." Sometimes it's something entirely different than you imagined. But one thing never changes: you are never turned away. The invitation is always open. Your voice is always welcome.

But somehow in growing up, we lose that boldness. We start praying like we're walking on eggshells. We ask with disclaimers. We hesitate, unsure if our longing is too much, or too little. We say things like:

"I know You're busy with bigger things..."

"I don't want to be selfish..."

"This probably doesn't matter..."

And somewhere in that cautious editing, we begin to believe a lie: That God only wants the important stuff. That our voice is a burden. That we have to protect ourselves from disappointment, even in prayer.

But childlike faith doesn't overthink. It doesn't manage expectations. It doesn't try to sound holy. It simply believes: If I care about it, my Father does too. And that's exactly what God wants—a relationship where we bring everything to Him. Not just the polished requests, but the vulnerable ones. The little things. The seemingly silly ones. Because trust doesn't overthink. Trust asks.

Confidence Before the Throne

Chessy asks for a fairy bedroom like it's a completely reasonable, logical request. She asks for rollerblades even though it's the middle of winter. She asks for pimple patches like they're treasure, because in her heart, if something matters to her, it's worth bringing up.

To Chessy, there's no divide between what's "spiritual" and what's "silly." It's all worth bringing to me because I'm her mom, and she trusts that I care about what matters to her. And maybe, like you, I sometimes want to say, "Chessy, that's not practical," or "Let's wait," or "We'll see." But the way she comes to me—with open hands and a hopeful heart—always softens me. Because it reminds me that even when I can't give her everything she wants, I love that she brings it to me anyway.

And if I, as an imperfect mother, love when she brings me her desires, how much more does our Heavenly Father?

In Luke 11:11–13, Jesus said:
"Which of you fathers, if your son asks for a fish, will give him a snake instead? Or if he asks for an egg, will give him a scorpion? If you then, though you are evil, know how to give good gifts to your children, how much more will your Father in heaven give the Holy Spirit to those who ask him!"

How much more? If I can look at Chessy's wildest wishes and still want to bless her, how much more can God? In Hebrews 4:16, we are told,

"Let us then approach God's throne of grace with confidence..."

Not fear. Not shame. Confidence.

Chessy doesn't come to me with a PowerPoint presentation or legal defense for why she deserves a dog. She just asks, because I'm her mom. And we can ask, because He's our Father. Not a distant deity. Not a grumpy taskmaster. A Father who delights in us and cares about the things that matter to our hearts, even the ones that seem silly. He's the One who numbers the hairs on our head, who hears our every whisper, who stores our tears in a bottle. There is no detail too tiny, no dream too whimsical, no request too outlandish for Him to handle with love.

So go ahead. Ask for your version of the fairy bedroom. Ask for the roller blades, the pimple patch, the dog. Ask for what your heart longs for. Not because you're sure you'll get it, but because you're sure He loves you enough to listen. And who knows? Maybe your fairy bedroom won't look exactly like you imagined. But maybe, just maybe, you'll get twinkle lights, a canopy bed decorated with leaves and flowers, and something even greater: the peace of knowing He heard you. Because the real miracle isn't always in what He gives. It's in the love that invites you to ask in the first place.

A Prayer for Bold Asking

Father,
Thank You that I never have to be afraid to come to You.
You welcome me with open arms and an open heart.

Teach me to bring You my desires without hesitation,
to trust You without conditions,
and to believe without complication—like a child.
Remind me that You delight in every word I speak,
that nothing I care about is too small for Your love.

Today, I come without filters or fear.
Today, I choose to ask—because I know You care.

Amen

CHAPTER 8

The Girl Who Carried a Promise

She was just a girl in Nazareth. One among many. No crown on her head. No stage beneath her feet. Just dust on her sandals, the scent of fresh bread in the air, and a heart quietly turned toward God.

Perhaps that morning had begun like any other. The sun yawning over the rooftops. Dough rising on a wooden table. The rhythm of routine beating gently through the house. She may have been stitching a tunic. Or carrying water with careful steps. Or laying out the morning meal, arranging bread and olives with quiet care.

But then—Heaven broke in. A light, sudden and otherworldly, splintered the stillness. An angel stepped into her world and eternity drew breath in her small, quiet room.

"Greetings, you who are highly favored.
The Lord is with you."
—Luke 1:28

She blinked. Heart racing. Breath caught.

Was she dreaming?

The angel stood unwavering, light pulsing like breath from another world. And Mary—frightened but rooted—stood still. The words didn't match the moment. She was no queen. She was no prophet. Just Mary. Ordinary. Unqualified. Unlikely. And yet, chosen.

The air must've felt electric, like everything familiar had tilted, like the unseen had stepped out of hiding. And Mary—though shaken—did not run. She didn't argue or negotiate. She simply listened.

"You will conceive and give birth to a son...
and you are to call him Jesus."
— Luke 1:31

A promise wrapped in mystery. A Son, not born of man's will but God's. A womb made sanctuary. A girl made vessel. And in a single breath, her whole life shifted. The rhythms she knew, the plans she held, the story she expected, they all unraveled.

God was not asking for part of her. He was asking for all of her. Not just her belief, but her body. Not just her song, but her surrender. And still, she stayed. No panic. No protest. No deal-making. Just a heart opened enough for God to fill.

"I am the Lord's servant," she said.
"May your word to me be fulfilled."
— Luke 1:38

Not "I understand."
Not "Let me think."
Not "Only if it's easy."
But: Let it be.

It was a whisper of wonder, a breath of bravery. She said yes, not because she saw the full picture, but because she saw the Painter. She trusted not the path, but the One who called her down it. That's the sacred strength of childlike faith—it trusts more in Presence than in plans. It doesn't require control to give consent.

Trust Without the Map

Mary didn't get a roadmap. No angel laid out how Joseph would respond, or how the town would talk, or how her belly would grow beneath a cloud of suspicion.

She didn't see the manger, the magi, the massacre of babies. She didn't know about Bethlehem's no vacancy. She didn't foresee fleeing to Egypt under the cloak of darkness. She didn't see the cross coming. Or the crown of thorns. Or the sword that would one day pierce her own soul. All she saw was God. And that was enough.

This is the essence of childlike faith—the kind that says yes without needing to see the ending. The kind that walks when it would be easier to stay. The kind that chooses obedience over certainty.

Long before the cradle, before the shepherds or the star, Jesus was held—first not in her arms, but in her faith. She made room before she made space. She welcomed the promise before she carried the proof.

Childlike faith does that. It doesn't demand a plan. It simply opens the door.

A Quiet Strength

Mary didn't need to be loud to be strong. Her courage was not in her volume but in her willingness to carry the weight of the unseen. She bore the world's salvation under her heart, while others whispered scandal. She walked with God in her womb while walking roads of misunderstanding. And when she sang—oh, when she sang— it wasn't the voice of a timid girl. It was the roar of surrender, the anthem of a daughter who believed the impossible was already in motion.

"He who is mighty has done great things for me,
and holy is His name."
— Luke 1:49

Childlike faith isn't a lack of awareness. It's a fullness of trust. Mary wasn't blind. She was brave. She didn't pretend the road would be easy. She simply believed the One who asked her to walk it. And that's the invitation for us, too.

God still comes quietly, unexpectedly, into the rooms we least expect. He whispers promises that shake our certainty. He asks for faith before sight. He offers miracles in seed form—asking only: Will you carry this? Will you believe before there's proof? Will you hold space for the impossible? Will you say yes before you understand?

Mary's story reminds us that God doesn't wait for the qualified. He looks for the willing. You don't need a title to carry a promise. You don't need a platform to shape eternity. You just need to be ready to say yes. To let the unknown be holy. To let the weight of obedience become wonder. To believe that surrender isn't small—it's sacred. Because sometimes, the most world-changing prayers begin in trembling hands and whispered hearts is "Let it be with me." And when they do, heaven moves.

A Prayer of Surrender

Father,
Make my heart young again.
Strip away the layers of caution, fear, and pride
until what's left is a faith simple enough to say yes.

Like Mary,
let me believe without seeing,
trust without knowing,
follow without needing all the answers.

When You speak, may I recognize Your voice.
When You call, may I not delay.

Teach me to hold space for the impossible.
To carry Your promise with trembling joy.
To be brave enough to believe—
that You can use someone like me
to bring heaven a little closer.

Here I am.
Let it be with me according to Your word.

Amen.

God doesn't wait for the qualified—
He looks for the willing.

CHAPTER 9

The Smile Before the Answer

It was one of those long afternoons when nothing seemed to settle. Leon was fussy. Tired, but not asleep. Hungry, but not eating. Restless, wriggling, letting out little whimpers with furrowed brows and clenched fists.

I tried everything. Rocking. Bouncing. Feeding. Singing. I whispered every soothing word I knew, walked laps through doorways and down halls like a mother on a mission—hoping that peace might be found somewhere between the living room and the bedroom. But he wasn't settled, because something inside him wasn't right. And he didn't know how to name it. And I didn't know how to fix it.

Still, I held him. Still, I stayed. I didn't have the answer, but I had my arms. I didn't have the solution, but I had presence. And for a while, that was all I could give. And then, like a sudden clearing after a storm, it shifted. He stilled. His wriggles quieted. His brow softened. His fists released their hold on whatever ache had stolen his rest. And then he looked up at me—and smiled. Not the kind of smile that comes from giggles or games. Not one coaxed out by silly faces or funny sounds. This one was different. This smile stopped time. It was quiet and sure, like a light coming on in a dark room. The kind of smile that says, "There you are. I see you. I trust you."

And what struck me most? He smiled before anything changed.

Faith That Smiles in the Middle

Leon didn't wait for relief. He didn't wait for the moment when everything was fixed or finally made sense. He smiled before resolution. Before clarity. Before comfort. He simply saw my face, felt my nearness, and that was enough. His smile wasn't born from understanding. It was born from relationship. It said, "I trust you even if I don't understand you." That— right there—is the posture of childlike faith.

How often do we withhold our trust from God until He explains? How often do we delay our worship until we see results? How often do we wait for the miracle before we smile? But Leon taught me something that afternoon. Something deeply spiritual and surprisingly simple: Faith smiles in the middle. Not when it all makes sense. Not when the pain is gone. But when the Father is near.

I thought of a verse I've known for years—but that afternoon, it came alive:

"Though the fig tree does not bud and there are no grapes on the vines... yet I will rejoice in the Lord, I will be joyful in God my Savior."
—Habakkuk 3:17–18

This isn't a praise that waits for progress. This is worship that dares to sing while the fig tree is still bare. It's not naïve praise. It's defiant joy. The kind that says: "Even here, You are enough." Even when there are no answers, no visible fruit, no resolution in sight. Even when the ache lingers and the fog won't lift. That's the kind of faith that rests in the arms of the Father and whispers, "You don't need to fix it all—I just needed to find Your face."

Leon didn't need a detailed explanation for his discomfort. He didn't ask for reasons. He just needed me close. And something in his small soul believed I would stay. Not because I had solved anything in that moment, but because I hadn't put him down.

That's the kind of faith Jesus calls us to: Not blind faith, but resting faith. Not denial of hardship, but trust in the One who holds us through it. We don't need to understand everything to be at peace. We just need to know we're not alone.

Childlike faith doesn't mean we won't feel the ache. It just means we know where to rest while it's healing.

We Are Already Held

That afternoon, I realized how often I treat God like a receptionist behind a closed door—as if I'm stuck in the waiting room of heaven, checking the clock, hoping my name will be called. Waiting for answers. Waiting for clarity. Waiting for relief. But I'm not waiting for an appointment. I'm already in His arms. Already seen. Already loved. Already carried. Even when my prayers feel like silence. Even when the ache has no name. Even when the wait stretches into weeks or years. He is holding me closer than I realize. And maybe, just maybe, that's enough.

Leon smiled because he recognized my presence. What if that's the smile God longs to see on our faces too? Not the one after the miracle. But the one in the middle of the mess—The one that says, "I know You're here."

I think heaven leans in when we smile through our questions. When we choose praise before the provision. When we find joy in nearness before we see the outcome. When we let our confidence rest in who He is, not in what He does.

In those moments, we become children again. Not clinging to clarity, but clinging to the arms that carry us. Not looking for answers, but looking for the One who never leaves.

And maybe the most powerful act of faith isn't the loudest declaration, but the quietest smile. The one that breaks through our tears. The one that doesn't demand to understand. The one that simply whispers without words: I trust You. Even here. Even now. Even before anything changes.

And I believe, that's the kind of smile that moves heaven.

A Prayer to Smile in the Middle

Father,
Teach me to smile before the answer comes.

When life feels unsettled,
and I don't know what I need,
remind me that You are near.

Let my trust rise before the resolution.
Let my praise echo before the breakthrough.

I rest in Your arms today,
and I choose joy.

Amen.

Childlike faith doesn't wait for the storm to pass—
it smiles in the middle, not because everything is fixed,
but because it knows Who is holding us.

CHAPTER 10

A Little-Known Girl Who Never Gets a Name

She never got a name. Not in Scripture. Not in scrolls. Not in song. No family tree traced behind her; no memories preserved. Just one sentence, tucked in the margins of a prophet's story.

A girl, carried off like dust in the wind, plucked from her home in Israel to Aram by soldiers who didn't care about little hearts or broken dreams. No mother's embrace as the gates closed behind her. No time to gather keepsakes or childhood memories. No voice loud enough to protest. And yet—Heaven knew her name.

She lived in someone else's house, served in someone else's kitchen, slept in a bed not her own. Her days were quiet. Hidden. Unseen. But faith is not diminished by obscurity. In fact, some of the strongest faith takes root in the shadows, where no applause echoes, and no audience is watching.

There, in the quiet corners of Naaman's household, her heart still pulsed with belief. Not in her surroundings. Not in her captors. But in her God.

When Faith Finds a Voice

Naaman was a commander of the army of Aram, well-respected and feared. But beneath the armor, under the accolades, he was suffering. He had leprosy—an incurable disease that no one, not even the most influential man in Aram, could fix.

And then, from the quiet corners of his household, her voice—the one no one expected—became the one that changed everything.

> "If only my master would see the prophet who is in Samaria. He would cure him of his leprosy."
> —2 Kings 5:3

That was it. Just one sentence. But it was enough. Because the power of a seed isn't in its size. It's in the life hidden within it.

Her words cracked open a door. And through it—healing walked in.

She wasn't the kind of person the world listens to. She had no title. No lineage. No credentials. She was young. She was female. She was a slave. In the eyes of the world, she had no voice. No standing. No reason to speak. But childlike faith doesn't wait for permission. It doesn't require status or stage. It simply believes, and then it speaks.

She had no guarantee she'd be heard. No assurance her words would matter. But she carried a truth too beautiful to keep quiet. And so, she offered it. Not with eloquence. Not with persuasion. But with the courage that only faith can give.

She stood to gain nothing. No freedom promised. No reward offered. No credit given. Yet her faith reached beyond her own story. It reached for someone else's healing. For someone else's encounter with God. Because real faith isn't selfish. It doesn't always ask, "What's in it for me?" Sometimes, it just speaks because it knows who God is.

Belief in the Midst of Brokenness

She had every reason to grow bitter. Every excuse to stay silent. She could have closed her heart and locked the door, told herself that if God were real, she wouldn't be here. She could have buried her faith beneath the rubble of grief and injustice. But she didn't. Somehow, her trust in God remained unshaken, even in a place of sorrow.

That's not childish faith. That's childlike faith. It doesn't deny the ache, it just dares to believe that even in exile, God is still good.

Naaman listened. Naaman went. Naaman dipped seven times in the Jordan, and came up clean. The story follows him. It celebrates Elisha. It marvels at the miracle. But long before the healing, before the cleansing, before the change, there was a whisper in a hallway. A small faith that dared to speak. A girl in the shadows who believed that God could still work wonders. One line. One moment. And the entire course of a man's life changed.

We don't know what became of her. Did she ever return home? Was she ever thanked? Did she ever see Naaman again? We may never know. But God knows. And He wrote her into Scripture—not for her fame, but for our faith. Because her story isn't about recognition. It's about obedience. It's about the kind of faith that doesn't need a spotlight to shine.

What if our most sacred callings happen in secret? What if the most lasting impact we have is made with words that no one else hears? What if our greatest offering is the thing we speak when no one is watching, to someone the world says doesn't matter, at a moment that seems too small to count?

What if heaven still listens for faith like hers? Faith that believes without seeing. Faith that dares to hope for someone else's healing. Faith that plants the seed, and lets God write the rest.

When You Feel Forgotten

If you've ever felt unseen, if your days feel hidden, your voice feels small, your efforts unnoticed, take heart. You are not forgotten. Not by the One who counts every tear. Not by the One who hears whispers in hallways.

He sees the prayers you pray that no one else hears. He honors the words you speak in love, without applause. He remembers the courage it takes to believe from the shadows. Because sometimes, God writes eternity with those the world overlooks. And He still moves mountains with the faith of a little-known girl who never got a name.

A Prayer to Believe Without Being Seen

Father,
Thank You for seeing the ones the world forgets.
For using small voices to speak big truths.

Give me the courage to believe like that little girl—
Not for attention or reward,
But because I know who You are.

When I feel invisible, remind me that You see.
When I feel powerless, remind me that faith is
never small in Your hands.

Use my voice to point others to You,
Even if I never see the outcome.

Let me trust You in the shadows.
Let me speak hope in quiet places.
And let my life, like hers,
be a spark that leads someone home.

Amen.

Sometimes the most powerful faith comes
from the most overlooked places.

CHAPTER 11

When God Takes It Away

It happened so fast. Leon had found a pair of scissors—gleaming, sharp, dangerous in all the ways he didn't yet understand. To him it was just another treasure in a world full of wonders. A new thing to discover. Something smooth and shiny to grasp, to figure out, to make his own. A toy. To me, they were a threat.

My heart surged. My feet moved before my thoughts could catch up. I crossed the room in breath, bent low, and gently pried the blades from his fingers. "Not that, baby," I said softly, though my voice carried the weight of urgency.

He looked up at me with those big eyes—confused, maybe even a little hurt. In his world, I had just taken something good away. He didn't see the danger. He didn't hear the warning bells ringing in my heart. Didn't know what could have happened if I'd hesitated. He just knew something he wanted was suddenly gone. And that I was the one who took it.

His lip trembled for half a second. But then—he smiled. He scooted closer, nudged my knee, and asked me to play. No grudge. No suspicion. No blame. Just trust. And I stood there, stunned by grace.

When God Says No

Leon never demanded an explanation. He didn't question my motives or interrogate my judgment. He didn't pout. Didn't protest. Didn't point to the scissors, asking for them back. He just leaned in. Because he knew me. And that was enough.

That's what trust looks like when it's untouched by fear. That's what love looks like before it learns to doubt.

How often do we respond like that when God takes something from us?

Leon believed in the heart behind the hands, even when the hands said no. And that's the kind of faith I want—not the kind that only sings when all is given, but the kind that rests when something is taken.

I've known those moments, too. Moments when something precious was pulled from my hands—a dream I cradled. A door I prayed would open. A relationship I thought would last. A season I wasn't ready to release.

I held tightly. I questioned. I wept loudly. I mourned what felt like the best thing.

But God sees what I don't. He knows the hidden blade inside the beautiful thing I longed to keep. He knows the cost of letting me hold it a moment too long. And in His mercy, He removes it. Not because He delights in our pain, but because He loves us too much to let us bleed.

> "No good thing does He withhold from those whose walk is blameless."
> —Psalm 84:11

If He removes it, it's not rejection. It's protection. Not punishment. But peace, disguised as loss.

What amazes me still about that moment with Leon wasn't how calmly he let go, but how quickly he came back. He didn't need time to analyze. Didn't hold me at arm's length. Didn't wait for a better offer. He simply returned. With joy. With laughter. With complete, open-hearted trust. He chose me over what I had taken. And that, I believe, is the heart of childlike faith: It doesn't stew in suspicion. It doesn't demand an apology. It doesn't replay the moment in slow motion, trying to find offense. It remembers love. It returns to arms that have never stopped being safe.

There was a sermon in Leon's smile. A message louder than any Sunday homily. Because isn't this the posture of Jesus? He offered love before we asked for it. Died before we said sorry. Reached before we returned. And still today, when we pull away, when we question, when we grieve the "no," He doesn't shut the door. He opens His arms. He doesn't explain first—He embraces. He doesn't demand understanding—He offers presence. Because the gospel isn't an equation to solve. It's a love to surrender to.

The Trust That Follows

So what do we do when God removes the thing we longed to keep? The job that felt like our purpose. The dream we prayed over for years. The relationship that held our hopes. The season we wanted to stretch just a little longer.

We grieve, yes. But we don't have to harden. Because behind the removal, there is still a face. The same face that rejoiced over us at birth. That wept at our wounds. That bore scars on a cross for our wholeness.

If we could see His eyes when He says no, we would see no trace of cruelty. Only kindness. Only mercy. Only a fierce and holy love.

So let that be enough. Not because it answers every question, but because it anchors us when the questions remain. May we learn to trust like Leon did. To come close again, even when we don't understand. To smile again, even with empty hands. To believe again, even when the loss still aches. Because the greatest peace doesn't come from knowing why—it comes from knowing Who. He is still good. Still near. Still worthy of our trust. Even when He takes it away.

A Prayer to Trust Again

Father,
Sometimes I hold on too tightly to what You've taken
from my hands.
I wrestle with the "why,"
and forget the "Who."

But today, I choose trust.
Not because I see the full picture—
but because I know You.

Help me return quickly.
Help me believe again,
even when it hurts.
Even when it doesn't make sense.
Even when all I have is the comfort of Your nearness.

Make my heart like a child's—
soft, surrendered, and quick to run back to love.

Amen.

Sometimes love looks like a 'no'—and faith looks like trusting the hands that close the door.

CHAPTER 12

The Boy Who Heard God's Voice

He was just a boy. Still rubbing sleep from his eyes. Still growing into his sandals. Still learning the sacred rhythms of life inside holy walls. He had been given to the temple before he could speak in full sentences—dedicated by a mother who once wept outside its gates, who once promised that if God would give her a son, she would give him back. And she did.

Samuel grew up in the house of God. Not in theory, but in reality. He swept its floors. Lit its lamps. Opened its doors each morning. He learned its routines and rhythms like the feeling of his own breath. He heard the prayers of priests. Watched sacrifices rise in smoke. Listened to the law read aloud, line after sacred line. But he didn't know the Voice yet. Not really. Not personally. Until one quiet night, the silence broke.

"Samuel."

He ran to Eli, the priest who had raised him. "Here I am," he said. "You called me." Eli shook his head. "I didn't call you. Go back and lie down." So, he did. But again, it came.

"Samuel."

Again, he ran. Again, the answer. Again, the confusion. And then a third time. A third call. A third response. And finally, Eli saw what Samuel couldn't: It wasn't confusion. It was a calling. God was speaking to the child.

What moves me most about this story isn't just that God spoke. It's who He chose to speak to. Samuel wasn't a prophet yet. He wasn't a man of wisdom or experience. He was a boy. A child. A servant in training, still learning the language of the sacred.

So why Samuel? Because his heart was open. Because his spirit was still. Because childlike faith is the kind that listens.

When the voice came a fourth time, Samuel didn't argue. He didn't question whether he was ready or worthy. He didn't analyze, or hide. He simply said the words that have echoed through the centuries:

"Speak, Lord, for Your servant is listening."
—1 Samuel 3:10

No resume. No ritual. Just availability.

God Still Speaks

We live in a loud world. A world of noise and motion. A world where stillness is uncomfortable, where silence is quickly filled, where voices compete for our attention and hearts get tired trying to keep up.

But children hear differently. They haven't learned to drown out the sacred. They haven't grown suspicious of stillness. They still lean in when something whispers. They hear wonder in the wind. They sense presence in the quiet. They listen not to prove anything, but because they're curious, and present, and unguarded. And maybe... that's where God still speaks.

Maybe you've wondered why you don't hear Him. Why prayers feel like they rise into a ceiling of silence. Why direction doesn't come easily, or clearly. But what if He's been whispering all along? Not through a megaphone, but in moments. A verse that lingers. A thought that won't let go. A quiet stirring in your spirit that feels too personal to ignore.

He still calls. Not with thunder but with tenderness and all He's waiting for is the kind of heart that says:

"Speak, Lord. I'm here. I'm listening."

Faith That Listens

Childlike faith doesn't demand the whole plan. It doesn't wait for every detail to be filled in. It just leans toward the voice. It doesn't insist on a spotlight. It doesn't need applause. It doesn't argue for clarity. It simply says yes. Yes to the whisper. Yes to the mystery. Yes to the God who speaks—even if we're not yet sure how to respond.

Samuel's moment wasn't about knowing everything. It was about knowing who to listen to. And that same Voice? It still speaks.

You don't need a title to hear God. You don't need years of spiritual training or polished theology. You don't need a seminary degree or a perfect track record. You just need a posture like Samuel's: Still. Soft. Surrendered. Because God doesn't look for the loudest voice—He looks for the most willing ear. And that kind of faith? It's not reserved for the seasoned. It's not restricted to the old. It's for anyone willing to pause long enough to listen.

So maybe tonight, like Samuel, you lie down wondering if God still speaks. You don't have to earn the answer. You just have to say the words:

"Speak, Lord. "Your servant is listening."

He still calls. He still comes to the small. And He still chooses hearts that are listening.

A Prayer for the Listening Heart

Speak, Lord—
even if Your voice comes as a whisper.
Even if it wakes me in the quiet,
or interrupts the ordinary.

Tune my ears to hear You.
Still the noise inside me.
Silence the doubt that says I need to be older, wiser, or more
ready.

Make my heart soft like Samuel's—
quick to respond,
slow to question,
eager to say yes.

May I never be so grown-up
that I forget how to listen like a child.

I'm here, Lord.
I'm listening.

Amen.

CHAPTER 13

Dancing in the Rain

The rain had just passed. The sky still wore its gray like a shawl draped over tired shoulders. The air hung damp and fragrant, like the earth itself had exhaled. Flowers bowed their wet heads and puddles had gathered like little lakes in the uneven corners of our yard. To me, it looked messy. Dreary. A day to stay in. But not for Chessy.

She burst out the front door bare feet, squealing as if God had personally prepared the puddles just for her. She leapt, splashed, twirled, and laughed as if the whole world were a celebration. Her hair flew wild, her dress soaked through, but her joy was unstoppable. I stood there, watching in awe. How do they do it? How do children carry that kind of joy? That kind of freedom?

Children seem to carry this secret—a way of seeing the world that transforms puddles into playgrounds, pebbles into treasures, and dandelions into birthday bouquets. They don't need sunshine to smile. They don't need the world to be tidy to celebrate it. They dance when it rains.

Somewhere along the road, we forget. Grown-up eyes grow weary, focused only on the tasks at hand. We hurry past the small moments, only counting the big. We overlook blessings because they aren't wrapped in grandeur. We step over puddles instead of dancing in them. We scroll past moments of beauty because we've been trained to only stop for the impressive.

But joy isn't found in the grand, it's found in gratitude. And gratitude starts with sight. Not physical sight, but heart sight. It's the kind of seeing that recognizes the gift in the things others ignore.

Jesus said,
"Unless you change and become like little children,
you will never enter the kingdom of heaven"
—Matthew 18:3

That's a sobering statement. He didn't say, "Add a little childlikeness to your life." He said, "Change." Become like them. It's a call to transform, to relearn their way of seeing the world. He was telling us to trade our grown-up blindness for childlike sight. Because childlike faith isn't naïve, it's aware. Aware of goodness. Aware of presence. Aware of wonder, even when the sky is gray.

Joy in the Middle of the Mess

Chessy didn't ask if it was okay to get dirty. She didn't hesitate to calculate the cleanup. She simply ran. Because the joy was too full to stay inside. And maybe that's where real faith lives—not in the polished, prepared spaces, but in the moments we're willing to be swept away. Not by fear. Not by stress. But by something as simple and sacred as joy.

Too often, we wait. We wait for things to settle. We wait for the skies to clear. We wait for the house to be clean, the diagnosis to come, the prayer to be answered. But joy isn't always a reward at the end of hardship. Sometimes, joy is a decision we make in the middle of it.

Faith doesn't say, "I'll celebrate when it makes sense." Faith says, "God is here—so I will dance now." It dares to smile with soaked hair and muddy feet. It believes the presence of God is more powerful than the presence of trouble. It leaps while it's still raining.

What if joy isn't meant to be postponed? What if the miracle isn't waiting for the storm to end, but in discovering the freedom to laugh while it pours? What if faith today looks like walking outside, unguarded—barefoot, vulnerable, wild with gratitude—and saying with every soaked step, "This moment is still a gift."

You don't need all the answers. You don't need a cleaned-up story. You just need to believe that God meets you in the mess. Because childlike faith doesn't stand in the doorway, wondering when it will get better. It runs into the middle of it—arms out, eyes wide, heart open. It twirls in the tension. It splashes through the sorrow. It trusts that if God allowed the rain, He's already made joy possible inside it.

Maybe today looks gray for you. Maybe puddles have formed where you only prayed for peace. Maybe the rain came quicker than you expected, and it hasn't let up yet. But friend, there is still joy to be found. Not because the circumstances changed. But because God hasn't. His presence is not postponed until the sun returns. His goodness is not on hold. He is here.

So go ahead. Let yourself smile in the storm. Let your praise rise through the puddles. Let your heart remember what your childlike self once knew: You were made to dance—even in the rain.

Prayer of Everyday Wonder

Father,
Give me eyes like a child—
eyes that find beauty in the ordinary
and joy in the messy middle.

Teach me to slow down, to see,
to celebrate what You've already placed in front of me.
Help me to not miss today
while waiting for tomorrow.

Let my heart be full of gratitude,
my hands open with wonder,
and my soul anchored in the truth
that joy doesn't require perfection—
just Your presence.

Amen.

CHAPTER 14

The Shepherd Boy and the Giant

He wasn't even supposed to be there. David had come to the battlefield carrying bread and cheese for his older brothers—too young to fight, too small to be taken seriously. While the warriors lined up in armor, David ran errands for his father.

But then he heard it. The voice. Loud. Mocking. Defiant. "Choose a man and let him come fight me!" The taunt of Goliath echoed across the valley.

For forty days, Israel listened. For forty days, no one moved. But something stirred in the shepherd's chest—not fear, not pride, not the insecurity of needing to prove himself. It was faith. Not the kind born from years of training or victories won in armor. But the kind that grows in lonely fields—where God's voice is the only one speaking, and His strength is the only thing standing.

David looked at the giant, then at the crowd frozen in fear, then back at the giant again.

"Who is this uncircumcised Philistine that he should defy the armies of the living God?"
—1 Samuel 17:26

He wasn't seeking attention. He wasn't trying to be bold. He was simply convinced. Convinced that no voice was louder than God's. That no enemy was stronger than the One who had always been with him.

That's childlike faith. It doesn't deny the size of the threat. It just remembers the size of God.

When Saul tried to lend him the royal armor, David obliged. But the weight was all wrong. It clanked and dragged and threatened to bury him before he even reached the battlefield.

He took it off. He chose simplicity instead—a shepherd's sling, five smooth stones, and a history of God's faithfulness.

David remembered the lion. He remembered the bear. He remembered being a boy with trembling hands and a trust that roared louder than his fear. No crowd. No spotlight. Just a boy and his God in the quiet, where faith is forged.

Childlike faith doesn't forget who showed up in the unseen. It carries yesterday's victories into today's battles. It holds God's past faithfulness like a shield. It believes that the same God who came through before... will come through again.

For His Name Alone

David didn't bring a sword. He didn't need one. He brought belief. The kind of belief that runs toward the roar, not because it's fearless, but because it knows Who fights on its behalf.

> "This day the Lord will deliver you into my hand... that all the earth may know that there is a God in Israel."
> —1 Samuel 17:46

That was the point. Not victory. Not headlines. Not proving himself. But pointing the world to the One who had always been enough.

Maybe today you feel like David. Too small. Too unqualified. Too ordinary for the battle you're facing. Maybe the battle in front of you looks impossible. Maybe the giant before you sounds louder than truth. But childlike faith isn't about size. It's about surrender. Even if your knees shake. Even if all you have is five small stones and one wild hope. Even if you feel like the least likely person in the room—God can still use you. Because the power was never in David's aim. It was in the God who guided his aim.

A Prayer for Facing Giants

Father,
Sometimes the giants feel too loud.
Too strong.
Too much.

But You are greater.

Give me the faith of David—
to remember what You've done,
to believe You're still the same,
and to run toward the battle with trust, not fear.

I may feel small,
but I know You are big.
And that's enough.

Today, I place my confidence not in what I have,
but in who You are.

The battle is Yours.
And I am Yours.

Amen.

Faith doesn't measure the size of the giant—
it remembers the size of God.

CHAPTER 15

The First Tears and the Arms That Held Him

It happened on a quiet morning—the kind of morning that tiptoes in soft and slow, where the light drips like honey through the blinds and nothing begs to be hurried. The kind of morning where peace doesn't shout—it settles, gently. The room was hushed, and so was my heart.

Leon had been trying to roll for days. First came the wiggles—those delightful, almost accidental shifts where his tiny limbs danced with potential. Then the shifting of weight, a sort of rocking rhythm that said, I'm figuring this out.

I watched with anticipation, holding my breath between each grunt and giggle. I cheered him on like he was attempting something monumental. And to him—it was. It was his world getting wider. It was courage taking shape. It was movement born of mystery and instinct.

Then, finally—it happened. With one strong push and a twist of will, he rolled. Just like that, he was no longer where he had been. His face lit up in surprise—eyes wide, mouth open— like even he couldn't believe he had done it.

I clapped, full of joy. I scooped him into my arms, kissed his cheeks, and spun a little in celebration. He had no idea how proud I was of him. How precious even the smallest milestones feel when you've watched someone struggle to get there.

His eyes sparkled with new discovery. He had tasted progress, and it was glorious.

He tried again minutes later—eager, confident, full of that boldness only children seem to carry without shame. But this time, the ending was different. This time, the floor met him sooner than expected. A soft bump. Not dangerous. Not even very hard. But just enough to startle him.

There was a pause. One breath. Two. Then came the crying. Not just a whimper, but a full sob—the kind that rises from somewhere deeper than pain. The kind that comes when the world, for a moment, doesn't feel as safe as it did before. When something inside says, that hurt more than I expected.

I rushed to him. I gathered him into my arms, pressed his cheek to my chest, and whispered, "It's okay, baby. I've got you." And in an instant—he calmed. Not because the pain was gone. Not because the floor became softer. Not because the fear had vanished. But because he was held. Because he knew he was safe.

That moment has never left me. Because isn't that what our faith looks like, too? We believe. We stretch. We trust enough to try. And sometimes, it's glorious—like the first time we say yes to God without hesitation. Like stepping into new obedience, new calling, new beginnings. It feels like flying. Like lightness. Like, yes, this is what I was made for.

But then comes the next moment. The unexpected fall. The disappointment. The silence we didn't see coming. The ache we thought faith would protect us from. And like children, we cry. Not because we stopped believing. But because it startled us. Because we didn't expect the fall. Because we thought it would be easier.

But this—this is where childlike faith reveals its quiet strength: Not in never falling. Not in perfect execution. But in knowing where to go when the ground gives way. In knowing who to call when the tears come. In running into the arms that have never once failed to open.

The Arms That Always Hold

Leon didn't stop trying to roll. He didn't declare the journey too dangerous or the risk not worth the reward. Because in his world, the fall didn't define the experience. The comfort did. He knew where safety lived. He knew where love waited. And that's the kind of faith Jesus invites us into. Not faith that never wobbles. Not faith that walks in perfect straight lines. But faith that rests in the arms strong enough to catch us every single time.

Psalm 18:6 says,
"In my distress I called to the Lord; I cried to my God for help. From His temple He heard my voice; my cry came before Him, into His ears."

That verse undoes me. Because it doesn't say my prayer had to be beautiful. It just says —I cried. And He heard. He always hears. He doesn't flinch when we cry. He doesn't walk away when we fall. He comes closer. He wraps His arms around us and stills the storm—not always the storm on the outside, but always the storm within.

The ground may shake, but His arms never do.

The Courage to Try Again

As I rocked Leon, his tiny heartbeat pressed against mine, something quiet and holy unfolded in the silence. His breath slowed, steadying in rhythm with mine. The room was hushed, but heaven felt near. And suddenly, I saw it with startling clarity: Faith isn't just the courage to move forward. It's the trust that when we fall—because we will—we're not falling alone. It's the certainty that Someone is watching, listening, ready to gather us before we even know how to reach back. It's believing there is comfort for our pain, healing for our bruises, arms for our aching. That Someone is God. And He is always near.

We often measure faith by progress—by leaps taken, ground gained, prayers answered. But children don't measure. They simply believe. Not in outcomes, but in presence. Not in performance, but in love.

Leon didn't wait to be brave before he tried again. He didn't count how many times he failed. He didn't hesitate because of yesterday's tears. He tried again because he knew I would be there. And that—more than skill or strength—is what moved him.

That's the kind of faith that stirs heaven. Not polished, not perfect, but trusting. Because childlike faith doesn't just celebrate the victory. It doesn't just clap for the roll, the step, the "yes that worked". It believes in grace when we stumble. Especially the stumbling. It knows that the arms that celebrate us when we soar are the same arms that catch us when we fall. They don't withdraw. They don't grow tired. They don't say, "You should have known better." They say,

"I'm here."
"You're mine."
"Try again, love. I'm not going anywhere."

Maybe that's the greatest miracle of all—not that we walk without falling, but that we keep walking anyway. That we trust in a love bigger than our missteps. That we run, even with trembling legs, because we believe in the One who runs toward us.

So, if you find yourself sitting on the floor of disappointment, if the dream feels distant, if the prayer still feels unanswered, if the last fall left a bruise that's still healing—breathe. You are not alone. Love is not far. And Jesus is not disappointed in you. He is with you. In the ache. In the silence. In the space between failure and trying again.

And when you're ready—not when you're perfect, not when you've figured it all out, just when you're ready—try again. Because grace isn't just for getting up. It's what gives you the courage to.

A Prayer When I've Fallen

Father,
I tried.
I stepped out in faith—
and it didn't go how I hoped.

Now I feel the sting,
the bruise of disappointment,
the ache of "what if."

But You don't turn away.
You ran to me.
You lifted me up.
You held me close.

So here I am again—
not perfect,
but present.
Not fearless,
but found.

Stay near, Lord.
I need You.
Always.

Amen.

CHAPTER 16

Held in the Dark

It was the middle of the night. The room hummed with stillness, lit only by the faint glow of a nightlight tucked in the corner, just enough to soften the shadows. The world outside had gone silent, wrapped in a hush that made the minutes feel longer. Then came the crying. Sudden. Sharp. Piercing.

Leon's little body was curled in his crib, his eyes wide, breath catching in those hiccupped sobs that only come from fear. He didn't know why he'd woken. He didn't know where the fear had come from. He just knew something felt wrong, and it scared him.

I moved without thinking. No questions. Just the instinct of love. I scooped him into my arms, whispering comfort, cradling him against my chest. He couldn't see my face clearly in the dark. He didn't understand what had startled him. But as soon as he was held, his sobs slowed.

He was still in the dark. But he knew he was held.

When Darkness Comes Uninvited

Some fears don't knock first. They barge in at midnight, pulling the blankets off our peace. They rattle the windows of what we thought we knew—about God, about ourselves, about the world. We find ourselves wide-eyed in the night of a diagnosis, a disappointment, a loss, or an unexplainable ache. And like a child, we cry—not because we're faithless, but because we don't know why. Because we weren't ready for the dark.

There are moments in life that feel just like that. Moments when fear wakes us from our peace with no warning. When the world that once felt secure suddenly feels foreign. When the quiet turns thick and the shadows stretch longer. And something inside us trembles with a childlike cry: What is happening? Why is it dark? Where are You, God?

We want clarity. We want the lights turned on. We want explanations that make the fear vanish. But sometimes, God doesn't flip the switch. Sometimes, He doesn't chase away the night. Instead, He comes near. And His nearness becomes the light we didn't know we needed.

Because that's what faith looks like sometimes—not understanding, not control, but surrender. Not the absence of fear, but the presence of trust. Not a roadmap through the dark, but the sound of His heartbeat close enough to still our own.

Even the Dark Glows to God

Psalm 139:12 whispers truth into our night-seasons:

"Even the darkness is not dark to You; the night will shine like the day, for darkness is as light to You."

That verse settles something in me every time. Because I've known the nights that seem endless. I've cried prayers that felt like they fell into a void. I've laid awake, heart aching for answers, for peace, for God to show up with a flashlight and a fix.

But the mystery of faith is this: He doesn't need to turn on the light to find you. He already sees in the dark. To Him, even our midnights shimmer with meaning. Even our confusion is not confusing to Him. He holds the whole picture when we can barely hold ourselves together. He doesn't flinch at our fear. He doesn't grow impatient with our trembling. He doesn't say, "You should be stronger by now." He just gathers us close. Wraps Himself around our ache. And whispers what He's always whispered: "I'm here. You're not alone." There's a different kind of strength found when you're too weak to walk. Not in the trying—but in the trusting.

Leon didn't stop crying because he figured things out. He calmed because he was carried. And maybe that's us too. Maybe the holiest moments of our faith are not when we're running with certainty—but when we're limp in God's arms, unsure of the way forward, but clinging to the certainty of who is with us. The dark didn't end. But the comfort began.

The Stillness of Being Known

What moved me most that night wasn't how quickly Leon calmed. It was that he calmed before anything changed. I didn't turn on the lights. I didn't remove the dark. I didn't explain the mystery. But I was there. And to him, that was enough.

That's the heart of faith—not a demand for answers, but a deep knowing: "Even here... I am held."

There's a quiet kind of peace that comes from being known. From being scooped up, no questions asked. From being comforted when no one else even sees the tears.

That's what God does for us. He doesn't wait until morning. He doesn't hold out for our maturity. He doesn't say, "Figure it out, then I'll hold you." He comes in the night. In the middle of the ache. In the place that scares us most. And He wraps us in Himself.

Luke 13:34 reminds us of God's desire to hold us:

"...how often I have longed to gather your children together, as a hen gathers her chicks under her wings, and you were not willing."

— Luke 13:34

The longer we walk with God, the more tempted we are to replace childlike trust with grown-up strategies. We search for formulas. We chase insight. We want to feel in control.

But childlike faith doesn't need a plan to rest. It just needs a Person. It's the willingness to say, "I don't understand this... but I know who's holding me." It's the kind of trust that doesn't flinch in the dark, because it's not focused on what's seen—but on who is near.

Leon reminded me that night: Sometimes the holiest thing we can do is simply let ourselves be held.

A Prayer for the Night

Father,
Sometimes the dark feels heavy—
not just around me, but inside me.

I wake to fear I can't name.
I carry questions I can't answer.
And I long for light that hasn't come yet.

But tonight, I remember:
You are near, even here.

I don't need all the answers.
I don't need to see the way.
I just need to rest in the truth
that I am held.

So hold me, Lord.
In this room. In this moment.
In this quiet, uncertain place.

And let Your presence
be enough.

Amen.

Faith doesn't always chase answers. Sometimes, it just clings to presence—and finds peace in the dark.

CHAPTER 17

A Crown Too Big for His Head

The crown slipped down over his forehead the day they placed it there. Too large for his still-growing frame. Too heavy for shoulders that had not yet carried even a decade of life.

Josiah was only eight. Too young, many thought, to reign. Too innocent to judge. Too inexperienced to be taken seriously. Too small to carry the weight of a kingdom whose grown men had failed to carry it well.

But heaven never waits for age to measure worth. God does not count years, He reads hearts. We crown with caution, but heaven crowns with purpose. We look for resumes, He looks for reverence. And in this small boy, God found something rare: A heart that leaned in. A spirit that listened. A will ready to obey.

While kings before him chased power, and others after him would chase applause, Josiah chased something older, deeper, truer: The face of God.

The Book They Forgot and the Boy Who Remembered

Years passed. The boy who had once tripped over his crown now walked with quiet authority. Not the kind that shouts to be seen, but the kind that bends to hear. And in the midst of his rule, something sacred was found. Hidden beneath dust, forgotten in the cracks of a crumbling temple, a book was uncovered. Not just any book—the Book. The Book of the Law. God's Word, buried beneath years of spiritual neglect and cultural noise.

When its words were read aloud, something in Josiah broke open. Not with defiance. Not with denial. But with tears. Josiah didn't respond with policy. He didn't consult his advisors. He tore his royal robes—not as a king making a show, but as a child who realized his Father had been grieved. A child heartbroken by the truth. Because the words weren't just ink on parchment. They were arrows—aimed with love and sharp with righteousness. And Josiah let them in.

That's the holy ache of childlike faith: It doesn't defend itself when truth arrives. It weeps. It repents. It returns.

He could have ignored it. Filed it away as relic, tucked it back beneath the stones of memory. But Josiah did what children so often do—he acted. He didn't just cry, he changed. He didn't just hear, he obeyed. And through his yes, a nation remembered God again.

Idols were shattered. Altars to false gods were torn down. Ashes replaced incense. Truth replaced tradition. And revival— true revival—was born. Not from a prophet's thunder. Not from a priest's ceremony. But from the obedience of a child-king who chose God's voice over every other.

Revival did not come through eloquence or experience. It came through the trembling obedience of a child-king who dared to believe God was still worthy to follow.

The truth is, true revival is never complicated. It begins with a heart that says, "We can't stay here. We must return."

A Slipping Crown, A Steady Heart

The idols Josiah destroyed weren't just carved images. They were generations deep. Traditions thick with compromise. Sacred to the people, though grieving to God. And it takes a rare kind of courage to break what others have bowed to. Even more to build something holy in its place.

But Josiah's heart hadn't been worn down by fear. He hadn't yet learned the language of apathy. He simply saw what was wrong, and in the simplicity of faith, he responded.

That is the gift of childlike faith: It does not wait for a perfect plan. It moves when it hears the whisper of God. It believes obedience is enough. Even if your hands are small. Even if your crown keeps slipping down.

God didn't choose Josiah in spite of his age. He chose him because of it. Because young hearts still hope. Because young minds still dream. Because young faith still dares to believe things can change.

Josiah's story whispers to us still: You are never too young, too quiet, too unseen, too unqualified to make a difference in the Kingdom of God.

Sometimes, it's the childlike souls—tender, trusting, trembling—who lead us all back to the altar.

The crown never quite fit Josiah—not the way others expected. But maybe that was the point. Maybe it's never about how the crown fits, but how the heart bows. And his heart bowed low.

In Josiah, we see what happens when a child says yes to God. When purity leads before position. When humility rules instead of pride. Because sometimes, the greatest leaders are the ones still growing into their call.

The crown may slip... but the hands of God do not.

A Prayer for Childlike Courage

Father,
Give me a heart like Josiah's—
young enough to be moved by Your Word,
bold enough to tear down the idols around me,
humble enough to repent,
and brave enough to lead others back to You.

Let me not be hardened by age
or dulled by the world.
Keep my faith fresh, eager, and ready to obey.

When You speak,
let me be quick to listen.
When You call,
let me rise with courage.

Teach me that revival doesn't start with crowds;
it starts with one heart surrendered to You.

Let that heart be mine.

In Jesus' name,
Amen.

CHAPTER 18

Like the Birds of the Air

Leon never worries about his life. He doesn't wonder if there's enough milk for tomorrow. He doesn't lose sleep wondering if his next set of clothes will fit him or if he'll have clean diapers tomorrow. He doesn't scan the pantry or pace through "what ifs."

He just lives. He wakes expecting nourishment. He climbs with confidence, trusting someone will catch him. He laughs freely, knowing someone will come when he cries. He stretches out his arms when he's tired, certain he'll be carried. He reaches for food without fear, because he's never known a day without provision.

He lives fully in the moment. Unaware of his dependence—but fully confident in it. He trusts, without effort, that he is cared for. And in that, he teaches me more about faith than any sermon ever has.

The Quiet Theology of a Baby

Leon doesn't carry backup plans in a diaper bag. He doesn't manage risk. He simply trusts the one who carries him. And that, I think, is exactly what Jesus had in mind when He said:

"Look at the birds of the air; they do not sow or reap or store away in barns, and yet your heavenly Father feeds them. Are you not much more valuable than they?"
—Matthew 6:26

Children aren't carefree because life is easy. They're carefree because they trust someone else is holding the weight. They don't ignore needs; they just know those needs aren't theirs to manage. That's not recklessness. That's childlike faith.

There is a holiness in how a child lives simply. Leon doesn't ask to understand every plan. He doesn't request a detailed timeline or tracking link. He doesn't demand receipts before he rests. He just lives his life knowing he is loved. And that might be the most faithful thing any of us could do: To wake up, and live as if we are cared for. Because we are.

The Illusion of Control and the Burden It Brings

Adulthood trains us well. We learn to brace for impact. To prepare for worst-case scenarios, just in case. We build safety nets, emergency funds, backup plans for our backup plans. We monitor, measure, and forecast. We call it wisdom, but sometimes, it's just fear in a nicer outfit.

We pray, but check the bank account before we exhale. We say "God will provide", but still lose sleep playing out scenarios. We surrender, but keep one hand on the wheel.

Meanwhile, the birds are still singing. Untroubled. Unhurried. Not because they've figured life out, but because they never tried to control it in the first place. And the children? They sleep soundly. Because they've never had to wonder if they're being cared for.

Sometimes I find myself spiraling—Checking numbers. Drafting plans. Rehearsing outcomes. Planning the future in loops that never land. And in those moments, I hear a gentle question rise: "Are you the parent in this story... or am I?"

Because if Leon ever began to stress over groceries, if he started to stress over shoes he hasn't outgrown yet, I'd know something was wrong. It would mean he'd forgotten what it means to be a child. Forgotten that someone bigger is covering him.

And maybe that's what worry really is—not a mark of maturity, but a signal that we've slipped into the wrong role.

The Hands That Always Provide

When Leon outgrows his shoes, I buy new ones. When the diapers run low, I restock without him even knowing. Before he can name the need, I've already moved to meet it. He never worries about how the provision comes—because that burden isn't his to carry. It's mine. And I am just his mother. Imperfect. Still learning. Sometimes stretched thin. But even so, I try to stay one step ahead—preparing what he'll need before he asks.

If I—flawed and finite—can do that for my child, how much more can the Father of heaven do for His?

God is never late to the shelf. Never short on answers. Never surprised by the size you just grew into. He doesn't wait for panic to rise before stepping in. He's already packing the next size up. Already setting the table for tomorrow. Already opening doors you haven't yet knocked on.

Provision was never ours to produce. Yes, we work. Yes, we plant. But we are not the source. He is. He sees the need before it's spoken. He answers before the question forms. And when He does, it's not with pressure or fear. It's with the gentle rhythm of peace. The kind that reminds us: We are held. We are covered. And we are never, not once, forgotten.

Childlike faith doesn't pretend everything is fine. It just doesn't let fear define the future. It doesn't drown in the deep end of "what if." It rests in the arms of "even if."

Even if the numbers don't make sense. Even if the waiting stretches longer. Even if the door seems closed. Even if the journey feels uncertain—God is already there. And He is still God. He is still good. And He is still holding.

What comforts Leon most isn't what's provided, it's who provides it. It's the nearness of someone who sees him. Who knows when he's tired. Who picks him up before he falls. Who shows up before he can name the need.

And isn't that what we all long for? To be seen. To be carried. To be known without having to explain ourselves.

That is the heartbeat of the Gospel: not that we have all we want, but that we are never alone.

Security Is a Person

Leon doesn't search the pantry for peace. He searches for me. Because peace, to him, has always had a face, arms, and a voice that sings lullabies over the chaos. And so it is with God. He doesn't promise stocked shelves or perfect plans. He promises Himself.

"The Lord is my Shepherd; I lack nothing."
—Psalm 23:1

Not because there's never need, but because there's never absence. He is always enough.

Jesus never told us to try harder, worry better, or predict tomorrow. He pointed to the sky. To creatures without barns or budgets. To beings who live without spreadsheets, but not without song.

"Are you not much more valuable than they?"
—Matthew 6:26

We are. And He's never stopped caring. So let the birds remind you. Let the children show you. Let your heart unclench and breathe again. You are loved. You are seen. And your Father feeds you still.

A Prayer to Trust Like a Child

Father,
You see what I can't.
You carry what I was never meant to hold.
And still, I try—
to plan it all, control it all, fix it all.

But today, I want to come like a child.
Hands open. Heart unburdened.
Not because everything makes sense,
but because I know You do.

Help me rest in Your presence
instead of reaching for certainty.
Teach me to trust again—
to breathe, to laugh, to live free
in the care of a Father who never forgets.

Amen.

Childlike faith doesn't look ahead in fear;
it looks up in trust—and find peace in the eyes of the One
who provides.

Epilogue

Still a Child

I began this book holding a child in my arms. But somewhere along the way, I realized—God was holding one, too. Me.

Every story, every stumble, every whispered prayer taught me more than I could've imagined. And as I watched my children live with unfiltered faith, I saw my own soul mirrored in theirs—fragile, dependent, and deeply loved.

This journey isn't about becoming stronger, braver, or more put-together. It's about becoming smaller. Simpler. More surrendered. It's about letting go of the heavy things I was never meant to carry...and climbing into the arms that were always ready to hold me.

Jesus said, "Unless you become like little children, you will never enter the kingdom of heaven." (Matthew 18:3) He wasn't giving us a cute metaphor. He was handing us a key. To joy. To peace. To Him.

So if you ever forget how to pray—just cry out. If you ever don't know what to do—just reach up. And when life feels too heavy, too complicated, too much—remember: He never asked you to carry it alone.

You are still His child. And He is still your Father. So live like it. Trust like it. Run to Him like it. Because the arms that held you yesterday...are still open today. And always will be.

About the Author

Eunike is a wife, a mom, and a writer who loves finding God in everyday moments. Through her writing, she hopes to encourage others to walk closely with Jesus in every season.